THROUGH THE JAIPUR JHAROKHAS

25 HANDWRITTEN REFLECTIONS

VAIBHAV SURANA

To our beloved Pink City!

&

To all my loved ones...

Contents

PREFACE

The act of writing about one's own city is an exercise in introspection as much as it is an exposition. ' Through The Jaipur Jharokhas: 25 Handwritten Reflections ' is a homage to my hometown, Jaipur—a city that is not just a geographical expanse, but a living, breathing entity with a personality as rich and complex as the patterns on its famous Sanganeri print fabrics.

Each essay in this collection is a piece of my heart, an attempt to encapsulate the myriad hues and shades of Jaipur's essence. These are not just reflections penned down on paper; they are a resonating chorus of my city's culture, and a canvas for my thoughts during the 25 continuous days I wrote them in.

In these pages, you will not find the usual chronological account of Jaipur's history or a guidebook to its famed landmarks. Instead, I offer you vignettes—glimpses through the decorative jharokhas, offering views that one can only see if they pause long enough to look beyond the surface. I wish to share with you the Jaipur that pulsates behind the vibrant façades, in the quiet corners where the true rhythm of the city can be heard.

This collection is also an invitation to wander, to explore, and to engage with a city that offers its tales freely to those willing to listen. The various things, persons and places that were the muses for these reflections, are sort of emanating their own unique essence under the warm embrace of the Jaipur skies, which tempts me to describe this collection as even a bouquet of assorted flowers from a garden.

As you traverse ' Through The Jaipur Jharokhas ', I hope you will feel the warm embrace of my city, vibe with its nostalgic lanes, and immerse in the spirit of its people. May these essays be an invitation for you to visit here and let your experiences be the threads that would weave a part of you too into the fabric of Jaipur.

With each page, let us now embark on a journey together—a journey not just through the heart of Jaipur but through the annals of history, emotion, and the human experience that this city particularly offers. Welcome, dear reader, to a chronicle of love letters to Jaipur, written from the depths of a heart that beats in unison with the rhythm of this age-old yet ever-renewing city.

-Vaibhav Surana

ACKNOWLEDGEMENTS

To all the known and unknown persons, who have crafted the tapestry of the Pink City as we know it today.

To my friend's niece Chiku who lent her beautiful handwriting to my essays, but that was of course in lieu of some chocolates, toys, and movie merchandise.

Also acknowledged that the illustrations herein were created using multiple licensed computer software. They may be inspired by a mix of real people, places and things; but do not represent any real entity in any manner.

I
Whispers In The Wind

19 January 2024, Friday
Whispers in The Wind – Ft. The Hawa Mahal

Perched above the vibrant streets of Jaipur, the countless windows of Hawa Mahal stand as silent custodians of time and tales. Known as the 'Palace of Winds,' this architectural marvel whispers stories carried by the breeze, tales that flutter through its intricate latticework like delicate saris in the sun. These are the whispers in the wind, the breath of the city, murmuring secrets of the past and present to anyone who dares to listen.

From the earliest light of dawn, when the sun casts a golden blush on its pink facade, the Hawa Mahal listens. It hears the soft patter of pigeons' wings, the distant clang of temple bells, and the gentle hush of the morning breeze. These sounds merge with the aroma of brewing masala chai and fresh kachoris, creating a symphony that narrates the awakening of the city. The palace's windows, with their honeycombed pattern, serve not just as a barrier, but as a sieve, filtering the chaos, allowing only the purest of the city's essence to permeate its walls.

As the day unfolds, the wind carries the hum of daily

life. The laughter of children flying kites competes with the baritone of shopkeepers in bustling bazaars. Hawa Mahal stands witness to the lives woven around it, stories of love and struggle, of dreams woven in the looms of tradition. It listens intently, never interrupting, its presence a constant in an ever changing cityscape.

When dusk drapes its velvet cover over the city, the palace observes the quiet retreat of life. Now, the whispers in the wind carry a different tone. They speak of the day's end, of the secrets exchanged under the cover of stars, of lovers' promises and poets' musings. Hawa Mahal, under the moon's soft glow, becomes a keeper of dreams, its silhouette a testament to the enduring spirit of Jaipur.

The whispers in the wind are not mere gusts of air; they are the lifeblood of the city, a dialogue between the past and the present, spoken through the lips of Hawa Mahal. And as night deepens, the wind palace awaits the new dawn, ready to listen, to whisper, and to sieve through the soul of Jaipur once more.

II
Midnight Symphony

20th January 2024, Saturday
Midnight Symphony - ft. The Jal Mahal

As the vibrant hues of Jaipur fade into the velvet of a chilly January night, the Jal Mahal, adrift in the calm waters of Man Sagar Lake, prepares to orchestrate a Midnight Symphony. This majestic water palace, with its serene reflection mirrored in the lake, becomes the maestro of an unseen ensemble, conducting a nocturnal concert conjured by the gentle tunes of its surroundings.

The symphony begins with a soft prelude, the gentle caress of water against time-worn stone, setting the rhythm for the night's serenade. It's a sound both soothing and eternal, the heartbeat of the lake, pulsating in harmony with the soft murmur of the night breeze. The palace, bathed in the ethereal glow of the moon, stands as a silent sentinel, its intricate architecture a testament to the artistry of a bygone era.

As the night deepens, the rustling flora around the lake lend their voices to the symphony. The leaves perform a delicate dance, choreographed by the wind, adding depth and texture to the melody. This rustling is not merely a sound; it's an ancient dialect, narrating tales of the winds that have traversed the Aravalli hills, whispering the secrets of Jaipur to those who heed.

The nocturnal fauna, discreet yet integral members of the ensemble, join the symphony with their unique cadences. The owl's soft hoot pierces the silence, a haunting solo that evokes the wisdom and mystery of the night. Frogs by the water's edge offer a rhythmic croaking, a playful counterpoint to the owl's solemn tune. The crickets and other critters too add their small but important background score.

As the symphony unfolds, each note, from the faintest rustle to the most resonant call, weaves into a rich tapestry of sound, narrating the story of Jal Mahal—a saga of elegance, tranquility, and the unspoken communion of nature. The palace itself, a steadfast observer through the ages, embraces these melodies, its walls resonating with the harmony of history and the present moment.

With the arrival of dawn, the Midnight Symphony gradually fades, its melodies dissolving into the first light. Yet, the Jal Mahal preserves the concert within its walls, safeguarding the nocturne until the world retreats from daylight, and the maestro of the night raises its baton once more. Each night is as much an ode to the years gone by as it is a hopeful call to the future, a symphony of subtle sounds, where Jal Mahal remains both the stage and the custodian of stories whispered beneath the stars.

III
Echoes Of Yesterday

21 January 2024, Sunday
Echoes of Yesterday: ~~Ft.~~ the Jaivana cannon

Perched atop Jaigarh Fort, the Jaivana Cannon stands as a monumental echo of the past. Forged in Jaipur's foundries, this colossal cannon is not merely a marvel of military prowess but a silent sentinel of history, its formidable frame a testament to the ingenuity of its era.

With each sunrise over the Aravalli hills, the Jaivana Cannon narrates tales from a fabled era of iron and gunpowder. It recalls the fervent heat of the foundry where artisans and blacksmiths sculpted this world's largest cannon on wheels, a symbol of the then kingdom's ambition and technological mastery.

The cannon recounts its days as a guardian of the fort, its mere presence deterring foes and ensuring peace. It remembers the awe it commanded and the respect it garnered, its formidable reputation a silent custodian of tranquility.

As the fort welcomes visitors, the Jaivana Cannon

observes the present weaving into its history, one day at a time. Tourists stand in awe, their gestures a silent tribute to its enduring legacy. Their curiosity bridges centuries, honoring the cannon's saga of strength and peace.

Under the starlit sky, the cannon contemplates its legacy. It reflects on the rulers who envisioned it, the craftsmen who forged it, and the generations that have admired it. Its narrative speaks not of war, but of peace forged from strength, a legacy of foresight that withstands time.

As a keeper of history, the Jaivana Cannon is more than a relic. It symbolizes the enduring spirit of Jaipur, a city where each stone and cannon narrates a rich saga. It stands as a testament to the Echoes of Yesterday, a chronicle of resilience and the unspoken tales of those who protected Jaigarh Fort.

IV
Shattered Reflections

22 January, 2024
Shattered Reflections   Ft. A piece of broken glass

Within the ramparts of one of the many fortified hills of Jaipur, a shard of coloured glass lies amidst the dust, a remnant of a shattered jharokha window from an ancient haveli. For over a century, this piece of glass had been part of a vibrant indoor panorama, casting hues of history and heritage through its multifaceted surface. But some years not too far ago, when human endeavors to drill into the nearby Aravalli hills sent tremors through the ground, the window could no longer withstand the vibrations. It shattered, scattering fragments of a bygone era across the cobbled stones.

This shard of glass, once a part of a grand design, now lies in solitude, reflecting the fragmented image of a changing city. In every jagged edge and every fractured line, there is a story—a tale of resilience in the relentless march of time. The shard whispers of the days when it was part of a magnificent jharokha, through which the golden sunlight filtered, casting patterns of light and shadow on the haveli's ancient walls.

Despite its broken state, the glass shard carries with it the burden of heritage - no longer the vanguard of excellence but preserved only by the kindness of the modern times. It has witnessed the ebb and flow of generations, the laughter and tears of countless souls, and the silent transformation of the cityscape. Even in its fragmented form, it continues to capture the essence of Jaipur—a city where tradition and modernity coalesce, "But at what cost?", it humbly mumbles.

As the sun traverses the sky, the shard still captures the changing light, its now unnoticed reflections a poignant reminder of the fragility of beauty and the inevitability of change. In the warm glow of dusk, it stands as a testament to the haveli's past grandeur, holding within its cracks the memories of witnessed secrets, grand celebrations, and quiet moments of introspection.

Shattered Reflections is not just a narrative of loss and fragmentation. It is indeed a poignant reminder of the impact of human intervention on heritage and culture. It reminds us that every piece of broken glass tells a story, and every reflection is a fragment of a larger, more complex mosaic of history, resilience, and hope. In the heart of Jaipur, the shattered glass of the jharokha window continues to await its final clearance, accepting its own fate but still wishing luck to its surviving brethren to keep telling the tales of the past as long as they can and as long as someone would listen.

V
Fragments Of A Dream

23 January 2024, Tuesday
Fragments of A Dream Ft. Sisodiya Rani ka bagh

In the enchanting expanse of Jaipur's Sisodia Rani Ka
Bagh, a withered petal gracefully descends from a
vibrant bloom, embarking on a solitary journey. This
delicate fragment, once an integral part of a
resplendent flower, visualizes for one last time, the
Fragments of a Dream in the tranquil haven.

The petal, gliding through the air, carries with it the
warmth of sun-drenched days and the tender caress of
moonlit nights. It holds memories of the garden's
symphony - the buzz of bees, the gentle flutter of
butterflies, and the soft rustling of leaves, all
harmonizing in nature's delicate balance.

In its delicate beauty, the petal had been a silent
witness to the lives unfolding within the garden's
embrace - the laughter of families, the whispered
promises of lovers, and the reflective solitude of
dreamers. Each moment, a vivid stroke on the canvas
of the garden's history.

Resting on the earth, the petal merges with the soil
from which it once emerged, embodying the perpetual

cycle of life and the poignant beauty of impermanence. It is a testament to the transient yet impactful essence of existence, where each ending heralds a new beginning. The petal's journey perhaps mirrors our own, a kaleidoscope of transient moments and cherished memories that together weave the intricate web of life. Or maybe we have it even better, for unlike the petal, you and I even wield the power to shape our own dreams.

In the serene ambiance of Sisodia Rani Ka Bagh, the petal's voyage is a silent symphony to the fleeting nature of beauty and life. It invites onlookers to savour the moments of joy, to embrace the fragments of dreams that, when pieced together, form the grand narrative of our existence. Amidst the garden's lush foliage and intricate architecture, the petal's story unfolds, a delicate reminder of the eternal dance between nature and the passage of time.

VI
Melancholy Melodies

24 January 2024, Wednesday
Melancholy Melodies Ft. A Manganiyar's Kamaicha

Tucked away in a delicately carved sagwan wood cabinet, an old Kamaicha lies in the home of a Manganiyar musician, its strings resonating with the Melancholy Melodies of a fading tradition. This ancient instrument, with its soulful sound and rich heritage, isn't just a medium of music; it's a vessel of a community's cultural legacy, each note a lingering echo of the Manganiyar's storied past.

As dawn paints the city in hues of gold, the Kamaicha now off its shelf is stirred, its strings vibrating softly under the old musician's touch. The music that flows is rich with the tales of the desert, of starlit nights and the vibrant life of the dunes. The Kamaicha speaks of generations of Manganiyars who breathed life into its strings, infusing each melody with the essence of their nomadic soul.

Throughout the day, the Kamaicha stands witness to the changing rhythms of life. It watches the new generation tread paths divergent from their ancestral calling, their steps echoing a different tune. Yet, each melancholic strain it plays is a bridge between the old and the new, a tender reminder of roots that run deep and traditions that once defined a community.

As the twilight embraces the city, the Kamaicha's melodies delve deeper, narrating tales of love and longing, of the vast, open desert and the intimate courtyards where it once crooned unbound. The music speaks not just of nostalgia and remembrance but of the subtle ache of a tradition at the crossroads, yearning for continuity in an ever-evolving world.

In the solitude of the night, the Kamaicha reflects upon the melodies it has shared, the souls it has touched. It stands as a custodian of a rich musical heritage, a legacy of the Manganiyars that teeters delicately on the brink of the modern age.

In the heart of Jaipur, the Kamaicha's Melancholy Melodies are a poignant ode to a fading art form. They are an invocation of the past and a hopeful ode to the future, urging the next generation to preserve the whispers of their ancestors. As the city dreams and the Kamaicha rests, its strings hold the weight of history and the silent hope for a melody that will bridge the gap between the yesterdays and the tomorrows.

VII
Ashes Of Redemption

25 January 2024, Thursday
Ashes of Redemption : Ft. A labourer's chulha

In a humble corner of Jaipur, the
smoldering ashes in a labourer's chulha
speak of quiet endurance and hope, embodying
the hope of eventual redemption. These are
not just the remnants of a day's cooking, but
symbols of a daily ritual, a testament to the
resilience of a family striving for a better
tomorrow.

As the morning sun beams over the many
palaces of Jaipur, the chulha's ashes hold the
warmth of the night's fire. They have done
their bit and transformed simple ingredients
into nourishment, fueling the bodies and
spirits of those who toil under the sun,
constructing edifices of luxury that stand in
stark contrast to their own humble
dwellings.

Throughout the day, as the labourer's family
bends and builds, brick by brick, the ashes in
the chulha cool down just as the hard

working bodies warm up to work through the day. These ashes perhaps also represent the sacrifices made, the energies spent as offering into a yagna of aspirations amidst the dust and din of the construction site. Each grain of ash is a narrative of hard work, of hands that shape the future of a city, even as they struggle to hold their own present together.

As the evening descends, the chulha is kindled once more, its flames a beacon of hope in the dimming light. The ashes mix with the new fire, a symbol of continuity, of the enduring cycle of struggle and sustenance. In this dance of flames and ashes, there is a silent prayer for redemption, for the dawn of a day when the labourer's toil transcends into a future of security and prosperity.

In the quiet of the night, the chulha's ashes bear witness to the labourer's dreams. Dreams of education for their children, of walls that offer warmth and safety, and of a life that holds promise of more than the day's labour. These ashes are also a blatant reminder of the city's contrasting realities, a mosaic of luxury and simplicity, aspiration and endurance. Maybe that's just how the world works. But should it?

In Jaipur, the Ashes of Redemption in a labourer's chulha are not merely the end of a fire; they are the glowing embers of resilience. As the city sleeps, these ashes again reminisce over the few victories attained through daily battles of livelihood, and over the contrasting lives of a city that is a torchbearer of royalty and culture, nurtured by the dreams and toils of its many determined souls.

VIII
Silence Between Stars

26 January 2024, Friday
The Silence Between Stars Ft. An old man selling
peanuts outside Jantar Mantar

In the shadow of Jaipur's Jantar Mantar, an old
man selling peanuts shares a tale of the changing
heavens. His voice, as weathered as the ancient
instruments behind him, speaks of a time when the
night sky above Jaipur was a grand canvas, adorned
with countless stars and constellations.

"Back in the day," he begins, his eyes reflecting the
flicker of nostalgia, "the stars were our
companions. We didn't just see them; we knew them,
each one telling its own story." He scoops a handful
of peanuts, offering them as he points towards the
sky, now dulled by the city's glow. "But now, it's as
if the stars are fading away, one by one, lost behind
the light of our own making."

He talks about how the city's lights, once few and
far between, have multiplied, each new bulb
dimming the celestial wonders above. "It used to
be a symphony of stars," he continues, "but now,
we're left with only the Silence Between Stars." His

words carry a weight, a sense of loss for the star-studded nights that once were a hallmark of Jaipur's skies.

The old man recalls how, during the quiet times of the COVID-19 lockdown, the sky reclaimed its ancient brilliance. "It was as if the heavens were reminding us of what we've been missing," he reflects. "The stars returned, and with them, a tranquility we'd almost forgotten."

Finishing his tale, he offers a gentle smile, his gaze lingering on the instruments of Jantar Mantar, pedigreed witnesses to the changing skies. "Maybe one day, we'll find balance again," he muses, "between our city's glow and the celestial glow above."

As you leave, the old man's story lingers in your mind—a pertinent reminder of the natural beauty that hovers just beyond the city's reach, waiting for the moment when the stars can once again light up the Jaipur night sky.

IX

Embers Of Hope

27 January 2024, Saturday
Embers of Hope   Ft. A baati roasting pit

A busy morning in Jaipur's walled city. There's a crowd built up around a famous eatery. A modest baati roasting pit in the eatery's front porch serves as a hearth of unity and sustenance, its glowing embers a symbol of inclusivity and hope. Here, the Embers of Hope do more than cook; they bring together people from all walks of life, offering warmth and nourishment to all who gather around.

As dawn breaks, the charcoal embers are gently coaxed to life, their warm embrace ready to cradle the baatis that will feed the city. "These embers don't discriminate," the keeper of the pit says, placing the dough carefully over the charcoal. Rich or poor, everyone finds comfort in the warmth of a freshly roasted bati."

Throughout the day, the pit becomes a hub of activity, as its embers tirelessly turn simple ingredients into a source of strength and connection. The rich, smoky aroma of roasted baatis weaves through the market, drawing in a diverse mileau of people. Each one finds a moment of respite by the pit, the embers serving a common thread in their varied narratives.

"This pit is like the mother earth," the keeper muses, his eyes reflecting the charcoals' gentle glow. "Mother earth never discriminates and loves every child equally." The keeper even gives away free baatis to the poor, disabled and any school going kids who would ask. "The dough is neither ever wasted nor does it ever run out. Now tell me sir isn't this pit of glowing embers just magical?" The beaming keeper of the eatery is imbued by great hope for humanity while singing praises for his humble earthen pit of glowing charcoal embers.

As the day fades, the Embers of Hope continue to glow, their warmth a steadfast promise of another round of shared meals and stories. They stand as an oasis in the bustling streets of Jaipur, a reminder that in the heart of the city, there's a place where everyone is welcome, where the warmth of the embers feed not just the body, but the soul.

As you can't help but return at night to have another serving, the baati roasting pit and its embers seem like a symbol of enduring hope and unity, a place where the simple act of sharing a meal becomes a celebration of life's plentiful bounty, under the watchful gaze of the stars.

X
Threads Of Destiny

28 January 2024, Sunday
Threads of Destiny Ft. Makar Sankranti - The kite
festival

An incident of much intrigue, an encounter atop one of
the old houses of the walled city, it was Makar
Sankranti, the sky had literally blossomed with kites,
each steered by majestic Threads of Destiny,
otherwise commonly known as the humble manjha.
These threads, vibrant yet strong, are more than mere
tools for flying kites; they represent the game of life
itself, perfectly showcasing the balance between free
will and fate, between steering and being steered by
the winds of destiny.

"The kite attached to the manjha is only a dancer to
the tunes of fate," an old kite flyer remarked, his
hands expertly guiding his kite. "We control its moves,
its twists and turns, yet we never truly know whose
path it will cross or whose story it will entwine with."
As kites soared and dipped, the threads wrote their
own saga in the sky, a vivid display of life's
unpredictable beauty.

During the festival, the air is always thick with
competition and camaraderie, as each flyer vies to

'cut' the other's kite, a playful yet serious reminder of life's inherent challenges and conflicts. Yet, amidst this game of skill and chance, there's a deeper understanding. "It's not just about winning or losing," the flyer continued, his eyes on the kaleidoscopic sky. "It's about being part of this grand canvas, where each thread, each life, has its own journey, its own story."

And even as the game unfolded with many twists and turns, the people of Jaipur would never forget to savour the sweetness of the moment, in relishing gajak, rewri and tilsakri, the traditional sesame treats that add flavor to the celebration. "These treats," the flyer smiled, offering me a piece, "remind us to savour life, to find joy in the simple things, even as we navigate the intricate threads of our destiny."

As the day gave way to dusk and the kites returned to the earth, the great thrills provided by the Threads of Destiny lingered on in the minds of flyers. In the skies of Jaipur, these tussles between kites and threads are more than just a festival ritual; they are a celebration of life itself, a reminder to steer with intent, to embrace the winds of fate, and to always relish the sweetness of the journey, no matter where the Threads of Destiny may lead.

XI
Lost In Translation

29 January 2024, Monday
Lost in Translation : Ft. Maharaja Public
Library, Chaura Rasta, Jaipur

Nestled in the venerable embrace of Jaipur's
150-year-old Maharaja Public Library, within
its time-tested walls, lies a collection of
ancient manuscripts, some barely holding
intact, but surely each one a jigsaw piece of
history. These pages, whisper tales from the
bygone eras, their silent voices narrating an
epic of human ingenuity and artistic flair.

"The delicate manuscripts are akin to
gateways through time," notes the library's
keeper, his tone steeped in awe. "They cradle
the intellect of ages, offering snapshots into
the melting pot of thoughts that sculpted our
past." Amidst the library's musty aisles and
the faint aroma of aging paper, these age-old
documents stand as guardians of heritage,
each one a shard of the past eager to unfold
its narrative.

This assortment, with its frayed edges and

meticulously conserved pages, offers great knowledge with potential for connecting language, tradition, and wisdom. Historians and scholars have been leafing through these relics to traverse beyond maps and dialects, venturing into a realm where one could enter the minds of residents of a different time. The texts, inscribed in tongues from Sanskrit to Persian, are not mere containers of lore; they are monuments to the mingling of intellects, to the dialogues that resonated in the scholarly gatherings and royal courts of ancient times.

"Each ink mark, each crafted symbol is a universe of thought," the keeper muses, eyes drifting across the manuscript-laden shelves. "But as tales shift from one tongue to another, from one era to the next, certain subtleties and expressions hover just out of reach, lending these documents their enigmatic charm."

As yet another day passes, the manuscripts of the Maharaja Public Library stand as silent sentinels of a profound intellectual lineage, albeit some slowly becoming lost in translation. They stand testament that the quest for comprehension and interpretation is a ceaseless conversation, bridging the old and the new, the known and the mysterious. In the pulsing heart of Jaipur, these ancient scripts are not just remnants of the past; they are fragile, living gateways inviting each reader to wander through the labyrinth of human contemplation and insight.

XII
Echoes Of Eternity

30 January 2024, Tuesday
Echoes of Eternity : Ft. The Nahargarh Fort

Perched atop the Aravalli hills, I stood within the weathered walls of Nahargarh Fort, surrounded by the silent witness of time's relentless march. There, amidst the stoic stones, the Echoes of Eternity resonated, carrying with them the weight of untold stories and the whispers of a bygone era.

As I wandered through the vast courtyards, the laughter and secrets of ages past seemed to seep through the cracks in the stone, each echo a reminder of the countless souls who had once graced these grounds. The fort, once a bastion of strength and strategy, now stood as a melancholic testament to the impermanence of glory and the fleeting nature of power.

The fort's silent corridors, where royal footsteps once echoed, now bore the quiet tread of visitors, each step a soft murmur against the backdrop of history. The fort seemed to sigh, its ramparts basking in the golden hue of the setting sun, a daily ritual that seemed to very appropriately honour the beauty and sadness of dusk.

In the solitude of these ancient walls, I felt the pulse of Nahargarh Fort, each heartbeat a reverberation of the joys and sorrows that had unfolded within its embrace. The laughter of children playing echoed the mirth of royal feasts, while the hushed whispers of lovers evoked clandestine meetings under the starlit sky.

As night enveloped the fort, the Echoes of Eternity grew more poignant. The fort, bathed in the gentle caress of moonlight, was a silent observer of the city's dreams and struggles. Its presence was a constant in an ever-changing world, a reminder of the enduring legacy of human endeavors, and the quiet acceptance of time's inevitable march.

In plain sight, the Nahargarh Fort stood not just as a monument, but as a custodian of lingering details, a sanctuary where the echoes of eternity gently reminded us of the intricate dance of life and the quiet strength that lay in embracing the transient nature of all that surrounded us.

XIII
Dancing Shadows

31 January 2024, Wednesday
Dancing Shadows Ft. A puppet show

Amidst a lively crowd at Chokhi Dhani, a village themed amusement park in Jaipur, the dancing, flickering shadows capture the collective gaze. On gently nudging through the throng, the source of this captivating display slowly becomes clear: a traditional Rajasthani puppet show, its artistry painting stories in the play of light and darkness.

The puppeteer, seemingly a maestro of this age-old craft, skillfully manipulates the strings, his hidden hands breathing life into the wooden figures. Each puppet, under his guidance, casts an enigmatic silhouette against the screen, their shadows gracefully enacting tales of folklore and tradition. The audience, encircled around the stage, watches in rapt attention, their faces illuminated by the soft, intermittent glow of lanterns.

As the narrative unfolds, the characters, simple puppets by day, transform into heroes and legends as darkness falls. Their larger-than-life shadows dance across the fabric, depicting scenes of bravery, romance, and jest. The dance of the shadows, in perfect harmony with the puppeteer's rhythm, weaves an enchanting spell, pulling the spectators deeper into the fabric of the story.

With every sway and leap of the puppets, their shadows mimic each motion, creating an immersive spectacle that blurs the line between reality and fantasy. The flickering light from the lanterns adds depth and drama to the scene, enhancing the mystique of the dancing shadows as they flit across the stage.

As the show reaches its crescendo, the connection between audience and puppets tightens, each twist in the tale mirrored by a collective intake of breath. The puppeteer's artistry is celebrated not just in the tangible figures but in the mesmerizing silhouettes that echo their every move.

When the final act concludes and the shadows retreat into the obscurity of the lantern's dimming light, the audience, with a round of applause still echoing in the air, swiftly shifts its attention. In today's fast-paced world, where attention spans are often fleeting at best, the crowd moves on, drawn to the next attraction, the next snippet of entertainment that Chokhi Dhani has to offer. The puppet show, with its dance of shadows and tales of old, becomes a cherished but transient memory, a brief pause in the whirlwind of sights and sounds that define the rhythm of modern life.

XIV

The Forgotten Key

1 February 2024, Thursday
The Forgotten Key : Ft. A locksmith at MI Road

On a bustling stretch of MI Road Jaipur, right in the middle of a melee of honking vehicles and chattering crowds, I was looking for someone to mend by bent brass key. By chance I stumbled upon a ragged looking locksmith's makeshift roadside stand, he himself looking like a relic weathered by time. The locksmith, an elderly man with keen eyes and a shrivelled face, claimed to be the keeper of a forgotten legacy, the last heir to a once-wealthy zamindar family from Bengal. Within his possession lay an artifact of the past: a rusty, old key, the supposed gatekeeper to his family's lost fortunes.

"The key," he began in a voice laced with nostalgia, "belongs to a time when my ancestors walked through corridors of opulence, their lives woven with golden threads of affluence and grandeur. But fate is a fickle master, and our fortunes dwindled, leaving behind nothing but this key - the last remnant of our once-glorious legacy"

As he spoke, the locksmith carefully presented the key, its metal surface etched with the intricacies of its time. He shared tales of a grand mansion in Bengal, where hidden chambers held immense riches and artifacts of a bygone era. The key, he claimed, was discovered by him in a secret compartment within a small drawer many years after his family left their ancestral abode. He said he had once seen his grandmother open a hidden tuck in a chamber of their mansion, that was full of shiny objects, with that very key. But sadly he could never find any trace of such a tuck within the ruins of his erstwhile mansion. "Or maybe I just haven't found the right address yet!", he adds yearningly.

The locksmith's tale was a lore of mystery, of riches and ruins. The key in his hand was more than a mere object for him; it was a symbol of hope, a testament to the resilience of those who hold on to the legacy of their forebears. Amidst the keys and locks that cluttered his shop, this key stood apart, a real witness to the locksmith's lineage and the unspoken promise of stories waiting to be unlocked. He proceeded to strike my bent key with two confident strokes. Voila! My work was done.

As I left the shop, the chaos of a busy MI Road enveloping me once more, the locksmith's story still held my thought. I had encountered the tale of a forgotten key, a reminder that every object, no matter how mundane, holds the potential to unlock the depths of human experience and when found by the right person, can give great hope even in the direst of conditions. Or maybe it was just a story to entertain his customers. I'll never know.

XV
Symphony Of Silence

2 February 2024, Friday
Symphony of Silence Ft. Samayik a Jain spiritual practice

On a tranquil morning, while watching some Jain monks passing by my house, I remembered my late grandfather's practice of Samayik, a Jain tradition that would unfold in silence, each session in fact a profound immersion into the Symphony of Silence. This ritual was not merely a cessation of speech and worldly activities but an inward journey, akin to the meditative depths of many such other spiritual practices across the world. Within the embrace of this stillness, an inner rhythm would gently emerge. As the distractions of the external world faded into the background, the subtle rhythms of the soul began to resonate more clearly—the heartbeat of thought, the melody of breath, the harmony of emotion. This was not merely the absence of noise; it was an active engagement, a communion with the deepest parts of oneself.

In such practices, one finds a space where the cacophony of daily life dissolves, allowing the intricate symphony of their inner world to surface. It is in these moments of isolation from the outer world that one begins to truly listen and observe the rich notes within—a pattern of thoughts, feelings, and intuitions playing in harmony. This process of tuning into the inner self is a cornerstone of India's spiritual heritage, signifying not just control over and comfort within the self but also a profound connection to the universe.

The practice of Samayik, much like other introspective practices such as the introspective silence of Vipassana, the rhythmic trance of Sufi whirling, or the mindfulness practice of Zen; offers a path to understand the complex layers of the self. Each layer provides clarity and insight, guiding one through life's tumultuous score with a sense of peace and purpose.

In these silent sessions of Samayik, as I watched my grandfather, I learned that silence is not empty; it is replete with the music of existence. As easy and promising it may sound but such disciplined practice is quite a task. And when one learns to embrace this Symphony of Silence, they shall become more aware of their actions and emotions, while also enjoying a much needed respite from all the 'noise' in the world.

XVI

A Sea Of Whispers

3 February 2024, Saturday
A Sea of Whispers Ft. A visit by Macron and Modi
to Jaipur's walled city

Recently this January, the usually bustling bazaars
of Jaipur's walled city took on a different rhythm
as President Macron and Prime Minister Modi
traversed its historic alleys. On this particular
day, the regular hum of commerce was replaced
by a quieter, yet equally profound, Sea of
Whispers. The stalls and shops, although absent of
their daily transactions, brimmed with
anticipation, the atmosphere charged with the
significance of the visit.

The bazaars, known for their vibrant symphony of
trade and chatter, held their breath. The whispers
that day spoke not of haggling or the day's earnings
but of the soft power and growing repute of India
on the global stage. Each silent stall, each
crowded pathway, was flush with the pride of
hosting leaders of great nations, a testament to the
country's cultural richness and diplomatic stature.

As the leaders' convoy moved through the neatly

lined streets, their path led them to a famous Kulhad tea stall. The said tea stall, usually a cacophony of clinking cups and lively discussions, transformed into a serene backdrop for an exchange of cultures and ideas. Over the shared warmth of masala chai in an earthen Kulhad, the whispers in the air spoke of unity, partnership, and the gentle diplomacy that was unfolding over a simple cup of tea.

The visit of President Macron and Prime Minister Modi to the bazaars of Jaipur was a narrative of respect and admiration, a chapter where the usual buzz of the market gave way to a more subtle dialogue. It was a day when the Sea of Whispers carried stories of India's heritage and grace, stories that would resonate far beyond the city's historic walls.

In the silent, expectant atmosphere of Jaipur's bazaars, every whisper, every shared glance that day, became part of a larger story—a story of divulging a nation's past and its promising journey ahead, witnessed by the crowded and chatty streets of the Pink City.

XVII

The Enigma Within

4 February 2024, Sunday
The Enigma Within : Ft. An old gemstone
workshop in Johari Bazar

In Jaipur's Johari Bazaar, amidst its bustling
by-lanes adorned with novel goods and abundant
artisans at work, lies a gemstone carving
workshop that holds a special place in my
memory. It was my maternal grandfather and
uncle, both veterans of the gemstone industry,
who first showed me this enchanting place
many years ago. I was told that the artisans
there made jewellery and crafts with rare and
highly prized gems that could be afforded only
by the most affluent people in the world. My
uncle used to tell me stories about the place,
peeling layer by layer the enigma within, in a
space where each stone whispered ancient
secrets and each tool held a story waiting to be
told.

The workshop, with its walls lined with
rubies, emeralds, and sapphires, was more
than a place of business; it was a dimension
where the beauty of mere rocks from the Earth
met the craft of human hands. My uncle, with

his keen eye for detail and love for a good story, would often spend hours discussing the origins and lore of each gemstone with an old carver there. The air in the workshop was laden with tales of distant lands and of superhuman skill.

Since my uncle's passing in the somber days of the Covid-19 pandemic, whenever I am around this workshop, it acts as a place of reflection and remembrance for me. The tools and stones, the unfinished stories my uncle left behind, they all carry a piece of his spirit, his passion for the craft, and his love for the intricate stories that each gem harboured within.

Now, as I step into the workshop, the enigma within takes on a deeper meaning. It's not just about the mysteries the gemstones hold; it's about the legacy of my uncle, his connection with the stones, and the stories he left in my heart. The workshop, with its tune of chiseling and polishing, resonates with his memory, reminding me of the times we spent together. There's an enigma within the human mind too perhaps, in how the machinations of the psyche attach unique stamps of significance onto even inanimate objects and places.

For me, the lingering memory of the workshop stands as a testament to the enduring bonds of family and the timeless allure of storytelling, and also grants a quiet comfort that even in their absence, our loved ones continue to shape our world, one gemstone, one memory at a time.

XVIII

Torn Pages Of Time

5 February 2024
Torn Pages of Time Ft. A Bhopa's performance

During the festive season of Teej, when Jaipur comes alive with celebrations and the spirit of heritage, I found myself amidst the ancient walls of the Amer Fort, drawn to the performance of a Bhopa. They are a community of priest singers and musicians. The fort, usually echoing with tales of royal bravado, was that evening resonating with the poignant strains of the Ravanahatha, played by the Bhopas.

The Teej festival had transformed the city into a canvas of vibrant hues and joyful melodies. In the jubilant fervour, the Bhopa's stage was set in the courtyard of Amer Fort, under the open sky where the stars seemed to lean in, in front of a lucky crowd listening to the ancient ballads of Rajasthan.

As the Bhopa began, the melodic sorrow of the Ravanahatha pierced through the mirthful air, commanding an arresting silence from the gathered crowd. He sang of sagas engraved in the soul of the desert, of love stories that blossomed in adversity, and of the eternal relationship between humans and the gods. Each verse was a torn page from the annals of time, brought to life by the Bhopa's resonating voice.

That evening at Amer Fort, the Bhopa's performance transcended the festivities of Teej, offering a moment of profound reflection amidst the celebration. His narrative was not merely a recount of the past; it was a living, breathing testament to the enduring spirit of Rajasthan, its people, and their unbreakable bond with the land.

As the performance concluded and the final echoes of the Ravanahatha faded into the night, I was left in a contemplative silence. The Bhopa, through his art, had not just narrated the metaphorical Torn Pages of Time; he had woven them into the fabric of the present, ensuring that the stories of yore would continue to resonate, reminding us of our roots and the timeless wisdom that they hold. In an august gathering, under the watchful eyes of Amer Fort, the melodious narrative of the Bhopa became a bridge between epochs, a melody that bound the past to the present, and the celestial to the earthly.

XIX
Serenade Of Nightingale

6 February 2024, Tuesday
Serenade of The Nightingale : Ft. The Central
Park

In Jaipur's Central Park, as the day slowly
starts to hide behind the night, an old Neem tree
gets ready for a special performance. It's like
the tree knows it's showtime again when the
nightingale comes around. The bird's song starts
soft and sad, then fills the air, like it's telling
stories about the good old days and the quiet
times in the park.

That Neem tree has itself seen a lot too, standing
there while the world changed around it. But
when the nightingale sings, it's like the tree turns
into a stage, with every chirp and trill telling
tales about lazy walks, moments alone, and
friends just sitting together without saying a
word.

The nightingale's music doesn't stay in the park.
It mixes with the sound of the wind in the leaves
and the distant noises of the city, making a song
that almost says, "Hey, even in this busy place,
there's something calm and beautiful if you just
listen for it." It's like nature's own way of
showing it's tough, always there, singing the same

old tune.

People come to the park to get away from their busy lives, but they end up stopping to listen to the bird. It's like everyone understands this isn't just another bird song; it's a moment where everyone, even strangers, just stop and listen together.

As the night gets darker and the stars come out, the nightingale's concert hits its high note and then gently dies down, leaving a kind of silence that sticks with you as you prepare to sleep. This happens every night in Central Park, and if you could be there to witness it live, you'd remember it, like a sweet sound that stays in your heart and mind.

Right in the middle of Jaipur, with all the trees and paths of Central Park, the nightingale's singing is like a little reminder of how life's beautiful parts are often the simplest ones. It's a song that's part of the day-to-day but also something special, a little gift from nature, there for anyone who takes a moment to listen and keep it with them.

XX
Wandering Through Mirrors

7 February 2024, Wednesday
Wandering Through Mirrors   ft. Jaipur Literature
Festival

Around this time of the year, amidst the historic
backdrop of the pink city, the annual Jaipur Literature
Festival transforms the city into a veritable literary
maze, as if Wandering Through Mirrors. More so with
each author, each book offering a reflection of the world,
tinted with the hues of individual perspective and
experience. Like a hall of crazy mirrors in an amusement
park, the festival presents a myriad of reflections, each
book a mirror that distorts, magnifies, or subtly alters
the image of reality as seen through the writer's eyes.

As you navigate through the crowds, the air pulsates
with the vibrant synergy of thoughts and words. Each
session, each dialogue at the festival is akin to stepping in
front of yet another mirror, that promises to challenge
your perceptions and broaden your understanding of the
world. The books, the true stars of the festival, are of
course like an array of mirrors, each inviting you the
reader into a unique realm shaped by the writer's
imagination, beliefs, and the silent biases that color
every narrative.

In this carnival of reflections, the task of finding the
truest image of society becomes a quest of discernment

and exploration. Each book, offering only a fragment of the larger picture, a piece of the intricate puzzle that is the human experience. It's through the accumulation of these fragments, the sieving through multiple mirrors, that you begin to piece together a mosaic that resembles the most authentic reflection of society.

The Jaipur Literature Festival, in its celebration of diversity and discourse, reminds us that the world is a complex web of intertwined narratives. Like wandering through an elaborate maze of mirrors, navigating through the plethora of stories and ideas requires an open mind and a keen eye, knowing well that the reflection in one mirror may vary from being deceptively similar to even being wildly different from the other mirrors.

As the festival draws to a close, the books and ideas linger on in your mind, each a testament to the power of words and stories in shaping, reflecting, and sometimes, altering our perception of reality. In this grand hall of literary mirrors, every reflection, every book, enriches your understanding, offering multiple lenses through which we can observe, reflect, and appreciate the multifaceted grandeur of human society.

XXI
Ink-Stained Memories

8 February 2024, Thursday
Ink - Stained Memories Ft. Old court records

In the storerooms of Jaipur's old courthouses, stacks of legal documents, each a bearer of Ink-stained Memories, tell the tale of the city's evolving justice system. These pages, though yellowed with age, hold the narratives of countless individuals whose lives came to the doorsteps of law. The faded ink on these documents marks not just words, but the footprints of Jaipur's societal journey.

Each file and record, from property disputes to intricate legal battles, maps the changing contours of justice and order in the Pink City. The petitions, affidavits, and rulings are more than just paperwork; they are fragments of personal stories, collective aspirations, and the relentless pursuit of fairness.

In these records, the common man's voice would be evident. Petitions written in earnest hand, appeals for justice, and letters seeking redress - each document is a testament to their faith in the legal system. The ink stains, accidental smudges, and official seals on these papers are not just bureaucratic marks; they symbolize the city's commitment to upholding rights and resolving conflicts.

The Ink-stained Memories in Jaipur's courthouses are also more than just historical records; for they reflect the city's pulse. Comparing older documents with more recent ones can even reveal the shifts in societal norms, the evolution of laws, and the city's adaptation to changing times. These legal chronicles are not just about the past; they offer insights into the present and implications for the future.

As each day ends and the courthouses lock their doors, the stacks of documents rest in silence. Yet, the stories they contain continue to resonate; a reminder that the pursuit of justice is an ongoing narrative. The ink on these pages may fade; but the stories, lessons, and the quest for fairness remain, indelibly etched in the fabric of Jaipur's history.

XXII
Lament Of The Broken

9 February 2024, Friday
Lament of The Broken   Ft. Chand Baori

The Chand Baori, with its intricate architecture and historical significance, stands as a testament to ancient ingenuity, at Abhaneri, near Jaipur. This stepwell, renowned for its depth and the precision of its steps, also carries the scars of history. The invasions by invaders like Mahmud Ghazni and later by the Mughals left their mark, not just on the physical structure but on the essence of what Chand Baori represents. The destruction of its artifacts and sculptures during these invasions speaks volumes of the cultural loss experienced over centuries.

These artifacts, now lost or fragmented, tell a story of a bygone era, a "Lament of the Broken" that resonates within the walls of the stepwell. Each missing piece and every damaged sculpture at Chand Baori and the adjacent Harshat Mata Temple adds to a narrative of resilience amidst adversity. The stepwell, beyond its utility and architectural marvel, also symbolizes the cycles of creation and destruction, echoing the transient nature of human achievements in physical form.

Despite these losses, Chand Baori remains a significant historical site, attracting visitors who are drawn not only to its architectural beauty but also to its storied past. The absence of the once present sculptures forces one to only imagine the original grandeur of the stepwell, a grandeur that was diminished but not extinguished by the ravages of time and conflict.

In reflecting on Chand Baori's past, the focus shifts from what has been broken to what still stands. The stepwell's enduring presence is a silent declaration of the lasting impact of cultural heritage, despite the inevitable changes wrought by history. It stands as a monument not only to the architectural and engineering prowess of ancient India but also to the resilience of its people and their ability to withstand the tides of conquest and change.

XXIII
Starlight Whispers

10 February 2024, Saturday
Starlight Whispers Ft. The Birla Planetarium

The moment I had first crossed the threshold of Jaipur's Birla Planetarium as a child, it marked the beginning of an everlasting intrigue with the cosmos. It was as though I had slipped through a secret passage, where the earthly and the celestial realms melded into one. As the dome's lights gracefully receded, the ceiling metamorphosed into a vast, star studded night sky—a breathtaking view of glimmering stars and distant galaxies that seemed almost within reach.

"Starlight Whispers," a phrase that had once lingered lightly in my imagination, transformed into a palpable experience that evening. The guide's voice, gentle yet utterly enthralling, wove the legends and stories of the constellations into a narrative so vivid, it felt as if the cosmos itself was confiding in us. It was as if each star, each galaxy, was leaning down to share its ancient tales and secrets, inviting us into a dialogue that transcended time and space.

Every constellation unveiled a secret, every planet a character, in this grand, unfolding saga of the universe. With each movement of the projector, as new celestial bodies came into view, my wonder grew. It was as though the universe was whispering directly to me, its voice carried across light-years and through millennia, in a conversation that stretched across the vast expanse of existence.

That visit was far more than a mere educational excursion; it was like a voyage that kindled a deep-seated yearning to explore the mysteries beyond our familiar azure heavens. The whispers of the starlight that evening, sowed the seeds of wonder in my heart, nurturing a relentless quest for knowledge about this enigmatic universe.

Years have passed since that memorable day, yet the memory remains etched in my mind with vivid clarity—a stark, indelible mark that serves as a constant reminder of when I first truly listened to the universe speaking. The Birla Planetarium that day, in its majestic simplicity, had offered me a portal to the infinite, transforming those ethereal whispers of starlight into a language my soul has sought to decipher ever since.

XXIV
Ephemeral Echoes

11 February 2024, Sunday
Ephemeral Echoes Ft. Jaipur monsoons and Peacocks

A Jaipur monsoon may last only for a short while, but it brings with it a beautiful mix of sights and sounds that feel like an open display of nature's insurmountable artistic flair. The raindrops too make their own music, falling on rooftops, streets, and leaves, creating a calming melody that's a welcome break from the intense heat of summer.

But it's not just the pitter-patter of the falling raindrops that add to the city's monsoon canvas. The distant rumble of the clouds, the sizzle of pakoras being fried, the washed views of forts and temples, the giggles of children splashing in puddles and even the sight of a rainbow over the Aravallis. They all add their unique flavours to a typical Jaipur monsoon.

Among these common sights and sounds, there's one more that really captures the magic of the monsoon: the dance and calls of the peacock. Peacocks are everywhere in Jaipur, from the palaces and gardens to the hills and fields. They are celebrated for their beauty and are a big part of the city's charm. When they spread their colorful feathers and dance in the rain, it's a sight to behold.

Watching a peacock dance during the monsoon is an incomparable experience. They move with such elegance, showing off their vibrant feathers in a display that's both mesmerizing and beautiful. Their dance is not just for show; it's a way to attract mates, but it does leave everyone who sees it in awe. This dance is one of the many fleeting moments of beauty that remind us of the joy and wonder that can be found in the world, even when the skies are grey. They're like a special gift, reminding us to seek respite in the simple pleasures all around us even in the darkest of times.

As the rainy season recedes in Jaipur, its fleeting delights leave behind a poignant reminder of life's ephemeral beauty. These transient moments, rich with the essence of nature's spectacular bounty, inspire a deep appreciation for the present. Even as the rains cease, the echoes of this brief, magical period endure, etching a lasting impression on the spirit of Jaipur and its inhabitants, of celebrating the transient yet impactful joys of existence.

XXV
The Uncharted Pathways

12 February 2024, Monday
The Uncharted Pathways

Venturing into "The Uncharted Pathways" of Jaipur unravels a narrative less known yet equally captivating as its famed monuments and bazaars. These pathways are not just physical trails hidden away from the tourist's eye but also metaphorical routes leading to the crux of Jaipur's evolving cultural and social landscape.

In the by-lanes of the old city, beyond the well-trodden paths to Amber Fort and Hawa Mahal, lie stories untold, crafts unseen, and traditions unfelt. Here, the true essence of Jaipur's heritage breathes quietly, waiting for the curious and the intrepid. An early morning walk through these alleys, reveals the city waking up in rituals of tea making, flower selling, and the opening of ancient shops, each a chapter from the daily lives of the locals.

"The Uncharted Pathways" can also be found

in the burgeoning art scene hidden in plain sight, where contemporary artists and traditional craftsmen dialogue through their creations, birthing a new cultural identity for Jaipur. It's even found in cafes doubling as art galleries, in workshops tucked behind nondescript doors, and in festivals fusing modernity with heritage, celebrating the new while honouring the old.

As we near the end of this exploration of Jaipur, may these musings serve not just as a means to conclude but also as fuel to kindle our curiosity for the myriad journeys that lie ahead. In fact, the metaphor of uncharted pathways leads us to the quintessence of life itself— a constant voyage into the unknown. For the residents of this historic city, like myself, every day is an exploration of new horizons, be it through rediscovering our heritage or charting new courses in our personal and professional endeavours.

Our beloved Pink City, with its blend of ancient glory and contemporary dynamism, truly encapsulates the spirit of discovery and resilience. Just as the city embraces its past while navigating the challenges of the present, we too find ourselves walking our unique paths, inspired by the legacies we inherit and motivated by the dreams we yearn to realize.

In closing, this book is an ode to Jaipur and to the spirit of exploration that defines us. May the tales of its past inspire our steps into the future, and may we continue to find our own uncharted pathways, both in this city's many lanes and by-lanes, as well as within the vast landscapes of our lives.

* Vive Cada Momento *

~ Padharo Mhare Des . .. ...

Thank You

See You Soon In Jaipur...